ONE-HAND GRABS AND GRIDDY DANCES

FOOTBALL'S MOST SIGNATURE

MOVES, CELEBRATIONS, AND MORE

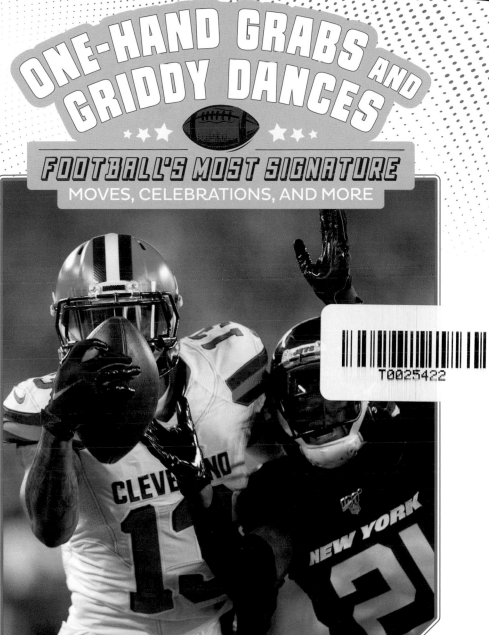

★★★★★★★★★★★★ by Steve Foxe ★★★★★★★★★★★★

CAPSTONE PRESS
a capstone imprint

Published by Capstone Press, an imprint of Capstone
1710 Roe Crest Drive, North Mankato, Minnesota 56003
capstonepub.com

Library of Congress Cataloging-in-Publication Data
Names: Foxe, Steve, author. Title: One-hand grabs and griddy dances : football's most signature moves, celebrations, and more / by Steve Foxe.
Description: North Mankato, Minnesota : Capstone Press, [2024] | Series: Sports Illustrated Kids: signature celebrations, moves, and style | Includes bibliographical references and index. | Audience: Ages 9-11 | Audience: Grades 4-6 | Summary: " Sports Illustrated Kids spotlights football's most signature moves and celebrations in this action-packed book for young sports fans. Patrick Mahomes' no-look pass play. Barry Sanders' jump cut. The Griddy Dance. These are some of football's most signature moves and celebrations! In this high-interest book, discover the history behind these iconic moves and many more-from the athletes who made them famous to their history within the game. Created in collaboration with Sports Illustrated Kids, Griddy Dances and One-Hand Grabs will have young readers and sports fans alike cheering for more"-- Provided by publisher.
Identifiers: LCCN 2023036619 (print) | LCCN 2023036620 (ebook) | ISBN 9781669065784 (hardcover) | ISBN 9781669065739 (paperback) | ISBN 9781669065746 (pdf) | ISBN 9781669065753 (epub) | ISBN 9781669065760 (kindle edition)
Subjects: LCSH: Football--Miscellanea--Juvenile literature. | Football players--Miscellanea--Juvenile literature. | Dance--Juvenile literature. | Celebration--Juvenile literature.
Classification: LCC GV950.7 .F72 2024 (print) | LCC GV950.7 (ebook) | DDC 796.332--dc23/eng/20230814
LC record available at https://lccn.loc.gov/2023036619
LC ebook record available at https://lccn.loc.gov/2023036620

Editorial Credits
Editor: Donald Lemke; Designer: Kayla Rossow; Media Researcher: Svetlana Zhurkin; Production Specialist: Katy LaVigne

Image Credits
Associated Press: Damian Strohmeyer, cover, 1, Kathy Willens, 14, Tom DiPace, 19, 21; Getty Images: AFP/Craig Lassig, 12, Betsy Peabody Rowe, 20, Elsa, 7, Jamie Squire, 9, Jeff Zelevansky, 23, John Grieshop, 27, Jonathan Daniel, 8, Kevin C. Cox, 10, Rischgitz, 4 (bottom), Sports Illustrated/Al Tielemans, 26, Stacy Revere, 5, Wesley Hitt, 15, 22, 25; Newscom: Icon Sportswire/Nick Tre. Smith, 17, Icon Sportswire/Nick Wosika, 29; Shutterstock: DarkPlatypus (dotted wave), back cover and throughout, Michal Sanca (football player), 4 (top) and throughout, wanpatsorn (football), cover, 1, wanpatsorn (football), 8 (bottom left) and throughout; Sports Illustrated: Damian Strohmeyer, 11

Printed and bound in the USA. 5626

TABLE OF CONTENTS

Signature Football 4

Sneaky Stuff 6

Getting Mossed. 10

Gotta Hand It to Him 14

Look, Over There!. 16

Run, Barry, Run 18

Reach for the Bleachers 22

Do the Shuffle 26

Viral Touchdown 28

Glossary 30

Read More 31

Internet Sites. 31

Index. 32

About the Author 32

Words in **bold** are in the glossary.

SIGNATURE FOOTBALL

Football began more than 100 years ago. It borrowed many rules from a sport called rugby. Today, these two sports have many differences, but they have one thing in common: teamwork.

A rugby match in the late 1800s

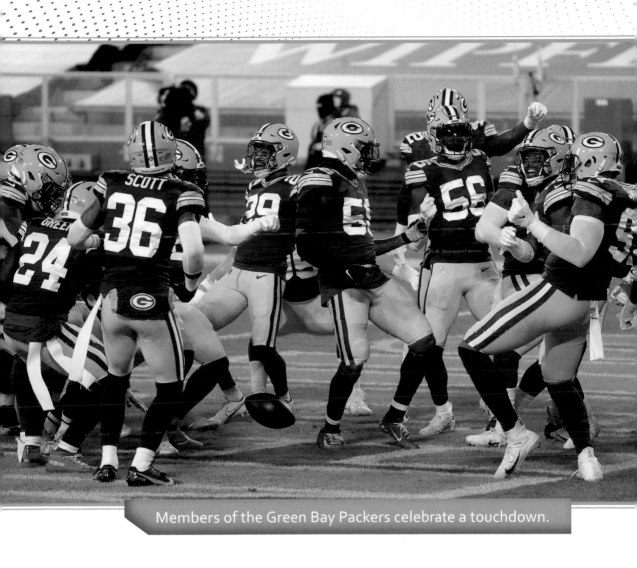

Members of the Green Bay Packers celebrate a touchdown.

Some football players become stars. They have special moves, cool **celebrations**, and their own unique style. They stand out from the rest.

SNEAKY STUFF

In football, there's a move called the quarterback sneak. The quarterback takes the ball. They dive or jump over the other team's line to gain a few yards. One famous player, Tom Brady, was a master at it.

The quarterback sneak is a super successful play in football. No other play has a better chance of gaining positive yards. In fact, the quarterback sneak works about 80–90 percent of the time!

Buffalo Bills Josh Allen runs a quarterback sneak.

For most of his career, Brady played for the New England Patriots. He ran a quarterback sneak in almost every other game he played.

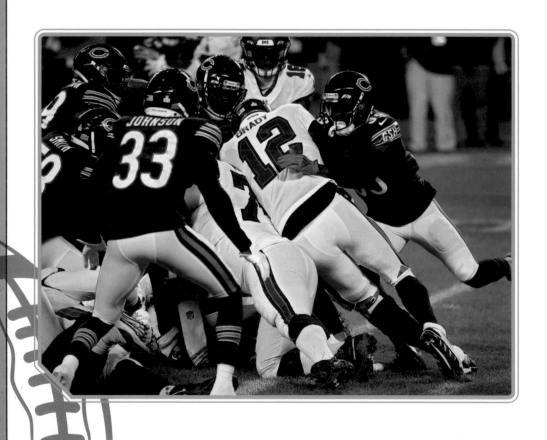

Brady (12) dives through the defense during a quarterback sneak.

The quarterback sneak is often used to dive into the end zone. The move helped make Brady one of the highest-scoring quarterbacks ever.

GETTING MOSSED

Randy Moss played for 14 seasons in the National Football League (NFL), most famously for the Minnesota Vikings. Moss is known as one of the best wide receivers in football history. He ranks second in all-time career touchdown catches.

Minnesota Vikings Randy Moss leaps for a pass.

At 6 feet 4 inches tall, Moss was very fast and known for his leaping skills. This helped Moss catch the ball above the reach of the defense.

Moss was also strong. He often overpowered his opponents. It's now common to call being overpowered for the ball "getting mossed."

RANDY MOSS
CAREER STATS

Touchdowns: 156
Receptions: 982
Receiving Yards: 15,292

GOTTA HAND IT TO HIM

Sometimes, a single move can change everything in football—even using just one hand!

New York Giants wide receiver Odell Beckham Jr. makes a one-handed grab.

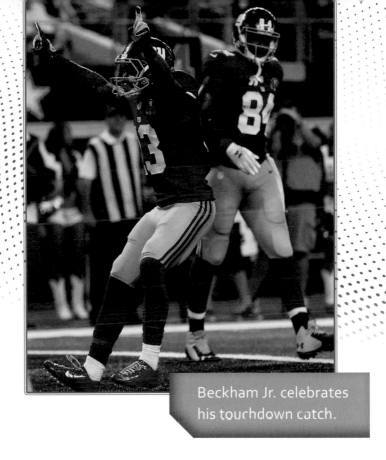

Beckham Jr. celebrates his touchdown catch.

In 2014, a rookie named Odell Beckham Jr. amazed everyone. He was a wide receiver for the New York Giants. During a game against the Dallas Cowboys, he jumped high and caught the ball with only his fingertips. People still talk about it as one of the most incredible touchdown catches ever!

LOOK, OVER THERE!

When quarterbacks throw the ball to their teammates, the other team tries to **intercept** it and take control. But guess what? Patrick Mahomes, a two-time Super Bowl MVP, does something amazing. He throws the ball to his Kansas City Chiefs teammates without even looking! It's like a surprise pass that catches everyone off guard. Only a skilled quarterback like Mahomes can do that.

Patrick Mahomes throwing a no-look pass in a game against the Tennessee Titans

RUN, BARRY, RUN

Running backs are the superheroes of the football field! They're fast, strong, and have amazing **endurance**. One of the greatest running backs ever is Barry Sanders. He played for the Detroit Lions from 1989 to 1998. Even with a short career, he left a huge mark on the game.

BARRY SANDERS CAREER STATS

Touchdowns: 109
Carries: 3,062
Rushing Yards: 15,269

Barry Sanders playing for the Detroit Lions in 1998

Sanders had a **signature** move called the jump cut. It made other teams go crazy. He'd change direction quickly, zigzagging all over the field. No one could catch him. Sanders was like a lightning bolt on the gridiron!

REACH FOR THE BLEACHERS

After scoring a touchdown, players show off their awesome moves. Touchdown celebrations are a big part of football, and some players are famous for their dances.

DeSean Jackson of the Tampa Bay Buccaneers

Victor Cruz of the New York Giants celebrates a touchdown.

One celebration, the Lambeau Leap, is maybe the most famous. It started when a Green Bay Packers player, LeRoy Butler, jumped into the bleachers after scoring in a freezing game on December 26, 1993.

Everyone loved it so much that it became a popular **tradition** in the NFL. When the league made rules about celebrating too much, they made a special exception for the Lambeau Leap because it's so unique and loved by fans.

Green Bay Packers Aaron Jones celebrated a touchdown with a Lambeau Leap.

DO THE SHUFFLE

In 1988, something amazing happened in football. Cincinnati Bengals player Elbert "Ickey" Woods did a special dance called the "Ickey Shuffle" when he scored a touchdown. The dance became famous. You might even see it on TV and in commercials.

Ickey Woods

Cincinnati Bengals Jeremy Hill dances the Ickey Shuffle after scoring.

VIRAL TOUCHDOWN

Have you heard of a dance called "The Griddy"? It all started with a high schooler named Allen Davis. He invented this dance and shared it on social media. It got popular and even college players started doing it. And guess what? NFL players joined in too!

In 2022, during the Pro Bowl, New England Patriots quarterback Mac Jones rocked "The Griddy" dance. He did it in front of millions of fans worldwide. It truly became a signature celebration.

Minnesota Vikings Justin Jefferson celebrates a touchdown by dancing The Griddy.

Football is full of exciting moments and signature moves that make the game even more thrilling. From amazing catches to dazzling dances, these unique actions add a special flair to the sport and capture the hearts of fans all around the world.

GLOSSARY

celebration (sel-uh-BRAY-shuhn)—a special action or dance performed by players after scoring a touchdown or achieving a significant success in the game

endurance (en-DUR-uhns)—the ability to keep going or continue doing something for a long time without getting tired

intercept (in-tur-SEPT)—to catch or seize something, in this case, intercepting a pass in football means catching the ball thrown by the opposing team's quarterback

signature (SIG-nuh-cher)—unique and characteristic moves or actions that are associated with a particular player and make them easily recognizable

tradition (truh-DISH-uhn)—practices or customs that have been passed down through generations and are considered an important part of a culture or group's history

READ MORE

Berglund, Bruce. *Football GOATs: The Greatest Athletes of All Time.* North Mankato, MN: Capstone, 2022.

Berglund, Bruce. *Football Records Smashed!* North Mankato, MN: Capstone, 2023.

Fleder, Rob. *Big Book of WHO Football.* New York: Sports Illustrated Kids, 2022.

INTERNET SITES

Pro Football Hall of Fame
profootballhof.com

National Football League
nfl.com

Sports Illustrated Kids: Football
sikids.com/football

INDEX

Allen, Josh, 7

Beckham, Odell, Jr., 14, 15
Brady, Tom, 6, 8–9
Buffalo Bills, 7
Butler, LeRoy, 24

Cincinnati Bengals, 26, 27

Dallas Cowboys, 15
Davis, Allen, 28
Detroit Lions, 18

Green Bay Packers, 5, 24, 25
Griddy, 28, 29

Hill, Jeremy, 27

Ickey Shuffle, 26, 27

Jefferson, Justin, 29
Jones, Aaron, 25
Jones, Mac, 28

Kansas City Chiefs, 16

Lambeau Leap, 24, 25

Mahomes, Patrick, 16, 17
Minnesota Vikings, 10, 11, 29
Moss, Randy, 10–13

National Football League, 10
New England Patriots, 8, 28
New York Giants, 14, 15

quarterback sneak, 6, 7

Sanders, Barry, 18–21

Tennessee Titans, 17

Woods, Elbert "Ickey," 26

ABOUT THE AUTHOR

Steve Foxe is the Eisner and Ringo Award-nominated author of over 75 comics and children's books including *X-Men '92: House of XCII*, *Rainbow Bridge*, *Adventure Kingdom*, and the Spider-Ham series from Scholastic. He has written for properties like Pokémon, Mario, LEGO City, Batman, Justice League, Baby Shark, and many more. His high school's football team had a four-year losing streak that only ended after he graduated.